DAGOBAH

This book is dedicated to everyone who wants to turn their dream business into reality. I know it's possible because I did it. You can too!

Back of the Napkin to...
Business Plan in 11 Slides

So easy you can build your
business plan on a flight
from San Francisco to New York

By
Brandon White

CONTENTS

How It All Started

On a fall morning in 1998 I was working at our headquarters and there was a knock at the door. My heart rate picked up about 20 beats and I thought to myself, "Did he actually come to see me?"

Here's what was going on: the day before I had received an email from a potential angel investor we were talking with about the possibility of investing in the social networking and e-commerce site for sport fishermen we were building. The angel investor explained that he was having lunch with a venture capitalist (VC) earlier in the day and as an aside they got to talking about what they did for fun. The VC said he loved to fish. The angel investor replied that he loved fishing as well and that he happened to be talking with my partner and I about the site we were building. The VC asked the name of the site and the angel investor replied, Worldwide Angler. The VC, with a surprised look, said he used the site all the time and that he wanted to talk with the founders.

The email from the angel investor said he didn't want to give our plan away, but strongly suggested I take him up on his proposal to make an introduction. With nothing to lose, I graciously thanked him for the offer and said we'd love an introduction. A few hours later I received an email that read:

> *Hi Brandon,*
>
> *I'm Tom and I just retired from Sequoia Capital. You might have heard of us—we've invested in companies like Yahoo, Cisco, Apple, and some others.*
>
> *I heard about your company during lunch yesterday with Matt. He had good things to say.*
>
> *I'd love to come see you tomorrow and learn more about your company.*
>
> *Tom*

Can you imagine getting an email like this? While one part of me was thrilled at this opportunity, another part questioned, "Yeah right, a partner from Sequoia

Capital, one of the most successful venture capital firms of all time, wants to come see me tomorrow because he's interested in our fishing site?!" Not that I didn't think we deserved it, but really, this guy was interested in us?

Heart pounding, not knowing whether to believe this or not, I wrote back:

> *Dear Tom,*
>
> *Thank you for the email and interest. I'd love to meet with you tomorrow morning.*
>
> *Attached is our business plan for your review.*
>
> *Our address is*
> *260 North St., Easton, MD*
>
> *If you have any problems with directions or anything else don't hesitate to email or call.*
>
> *Brandon*
>
> *PS: Bring some warm clothes in case we go fishing.*

That's how the knock at the door happened. I walked downstairs and opened the door, stared at the guy and said,

"Hi, I'm Brandon," as I stretched out my hand to shake his. Tom says, "Hi Brandon, I'm Tom," while shaking hands with a slight grin on his face as if some part of me had let on this was just a little surreal.

"Nice to meet you. Welcome," I replied.

Tom came in, I thanked him for driving over to see us and about a minute into the conversation Tom asked about our office and suggested we head over to it.

"That's a great idea," I exclaimed without missing a beat. I turned and started walking up our creaky hardwood pine stairs and motioned to him to follow. When I turned to see if he was coming I saw his grin had turned into a perplexed look. I turned around and kept going up the stairs a little more nervously than before.

I led him into the spare bedroom in our house. You'll remember I said I was working at our HQ office earlier in this story. HQ was code word for spare bedroom.

At this point in my life my then girlfriend, now wife, and I had scraped together every last cent we had to buy our small house for $108,000 not far from downtown Easton, MD. It was built in 1907, sturdy as an ox, but it was far from big and definitely not fancy.

Tom walks into our "HQ office," pauses, looks around slowly, and scans the two desks we had against the wall facing the street, the whiteboard on an easel in the back right corner that had our business diagramed, the small fly tying desk, and another table with a printer on it against the back wall that divided our headquarters from our sleeping quarters, aka our bedroom.

As Tom takes in this scene I realize he probably expected a "real" office, something more substantial that a Silicon Valley startup might have. Before I could get out a word in self-defense Tom asks, "Is this it?"

I didn't have time to panic, and without missing a beat I replied, "Well, my partner works out of his spare bedroom that he turned into an office down the road. We can go see it you want?"

At this point I'm convinced Tom showed up with much higher expectations and any hopes of him helping us were quickly fading. So, believing I knew what was going on in this moment, I said, "You came here expecting a lot more and I'm really sorry you drove all the way from D.C. this morning. Maybe I should have explained where we were in more detail when I emailed you back. I'm really..."

Tom interrupted me immediately, "Hey man, relax. It's okay. I've been using your site and you look a lot bigger from the outside. I'm surprised you can run the site from this room. I'm impressed. You don't have to apologize. This is how we found Cisco. They were making routers in their living room."

Writing that still raises the hair on my arms. Tom probably didn't realize how that simple reassurance affected me, or maybe he did and that was the point in him saying it. Now that we've been close friends for over 22 years, I now know he's way too smart for it to have been unintentional. Of course he meant it. He's probably reading this right now with a smile and letting out the gentle laugh he gives when you've figured out something that he already knew. But he knew you needed it figure it out on your own for it to have had a meaningful impact.

> **"You have to believe you can do the thing you don't think you can do."**

I remember that feeling like it was only a moment ago, full of unbridled confidence, optimism, doubt, fear, and courage all at once. When people ask me what it takes to be an entrepreneur, intrapreneur, or simply, a risk taker? My response is plainly, "You have to believe you can do the thing you don't think you can do."

At first glance that doesn't make any sense. In fact, it makes about as much sense as feeling unbridled confidence, optimism, doubt, fear, and courage at the same time. But that's what it feels like and that's what it takes.

If you're an experienced business owner, seasoned corporate manager, or executive, and you're reading this to launch a new product or service or you're looking to raise money externally or internally you know this is true.

If you're reading this as an aspiring entrepreneur or intrapreneur, it will make sense—trust me. Being an entrepreneur is incredibly hard, not because the fundamentals of business are hard to understand, but because when they say it's a marathon, not a race, they're lying to you.

A marathon is long, but entrepreneurship is a lifetime of marathons back to back to back— and it will test every ounce of courage, grit, confidence, and instinct that you have.

That's not intended to discourage you— in fact, quite the opposite. While this profession regularly tests my will and scares the shit out of me, I can't fathom doing anything else.

You'll feel the same and you'll have some of the edge taken off because the template in this book increases your chances of success. It's my goal to help you succeed!

Having someone with Tom's experience standing in your spare bedroom telling you that you look way bigger and badder than you thought you were gives you a kind of hope that's hard to explain, regardless of whether you're doing your first company, your third, or launching a new product or service for the first or fiftieth time. That vote of confidence irrefutably proves that success is possible. It makes all the difference in those moments of weakness when, instead of keeping on, you are tempted to quit. Every company starts with an idea on the back of a napkin in a spare bedroom, garage, or at the kitchen table.

The reality that Cisco, one of the most successful companies in the history of tech, much less any business, started in a living room, tells the real story of how companies get started. At one point, Cisco was just a few real people, just like the rest of us, and that truth brings so much motivation and confidence that with enough hard work anyone can build a wildly successful company. When you feel down, and you will if you haven't already, remind yourself,

"If someone else can make a wildly successful company happen in their spare bedroom, I absolutely can too."

But back to the story...

My tension gone, I started to explain to Tom how we did everything. From rigging up the phone system to sound like we had a bigger office, to what software we were writing—remember this is the internet in 1998. We were still working with flat HTML files. This meant we were handwriting on paper, using white out and sticking it together with Scotch tape versus using Microsoft Word or Google Docs.

After explaining how things worked and answering some questions I suggested we head to lunch. We jumped in the car for the three-minute drive to downtown Easton, MD to Washington Street Pub, a local hangout that wasn't too fast food or too fancy.

Once we ordered, Tom flipped over a napkin and started writing. I remember it like it was yesterday, his pen's ink bled into the paper slightly as he wrote. He jotted four things down with plenty of space between each one:

1. Product
2. Market
3 People
4. Financing

When he was finished he said, "Let's fill this in." By the time we got to "market" lunch was served. We continued working through "market," "people," and "financing" while we ate some good pub food.

These four areas would become the basis of the modern day business plan that I've developed through success and failure over the last 20 years. It's the plan you'll learn how to quickly create for your business, product, or service using this book.

Once we filled in everything and discussed it, we'd finished eating. Since things seemed to be going smoothly, I suggested we go fishing. Tom accepted enthusiastically.

We paid the bill and headed back to "HQ" to hook up my 21ft Parker center console boat. Then we grabbed some rods and fishing tackle and in just a few minutes we were headed to the ramp.

We launched and took a 30-minute ride to a high percentage spot (HPS), rigged up, and no sooner had our lines been cast, we hooked some Chesapeake Bay rockfish (aka striped bass). We fished for about three hours with steady action before we called it a good day and headed back to the ramp.

On the drive back, Tom asked me how much money we had in our bank account. I said I wasn't sure. He responded, "Why not?"

I explained that we traded stocks to help fund the company. He shook his head as if he wasn't sure he heard me right. I interpreted the headshake as an invitation to explain further and acted as if it was just a normal thing.

I went on to tell him that besides building websites for people, we mainly traded stocks to fund the company, and frankly speaking, we did really well. Ah, the internet heydays (I'm laughing while writing this).

Tom gives another nod. The one you get when a person is trying to communicate that they heard what you said, but don't necessarily approve of it or can't even believe you're actually doing it.

He doesn't say anything and I keep driving. A minute or two later he pulls out a checkbook. I see the spine and that about half the checks are gone, but keep an eye on the road since I'm pulling a 21ft boat at 65 miles per hour down a major highway.

Out of the corner of my eye I catch him handing me something. I look down and it's a check, he said,

"Here, let's go."

Curious, I took the check, brought my eyes back to the road to make sure we were still on it, and once I made a slight steering correction, looked backed down to read it.

It's a check for $50,000. I look over at him and he says, "Let's go—but, no trading with that money" half laughing, but completely serious at the same time. I reached over and shook his hand.

And that's how you raise money. Just kidding—well, not really, because that's how it started for me.

Here's a picture of Tom from that exact day, just in case you thought I was making this up.

The story of Worldwide Angler is as good as a big fish story, the one that almost got away. A story during the dot-com boom of the late 1990s with twists, turns, highs, lows, even lower lows, some redemption and ultimately success. But it's not one for this book. I'll put it in another book, or maybe I'll tell you over a bike ride if you catch me riding down Rt. 1 on the Northern California coast that we now call home.

What's important about this story is that while working and raising money for the business the way I did seems like it's out of the blue, it wasn't. It happened because I had a business plan that clearly communicated why people needed our product, what our product was, how it worked, how we were going to market it, make money, and how we planned on financing it.

Back then business plans were long form. They were painful to write, averaged over 40 pages, and felt more like a thesis than something you could use to guide your company. I learned how to write my first business plan in 1996 from a book I bought from the Barnes & Noble in Annapolis, MD. The irony of the whole thing was that book itself was several hundred pages. It took longer to read and learn what they were saying than it did to actually write the business plan. At least it felt that way at the time. Thinking back, it took me months to write that business plan.

Who has months to get an idea on paper before they start the work? No one—it's a waste time. Thank goodness times have changed.

While old school business plans can be complicated and downright intimidating, the modern business plan outlined in this book allows you to complete a first draft on a plane ride from San Francisco to New York. It's not only easier to create, it's dynamic. This plan is easier to change so you can keep up with the current market conditions of your business, product or service. Use it as a road map you can benchmark against.

"Here's a really cool thing about this: you can **use this modern business plan for any type of business.**"

This format took me about 15 years to develop because it needed testing. The market needed to accept that short doesn't mean incomplete and the format needed to be tested to see if people could easily complete it with my template and directions.

This is not do as I say, not as I do. I personally used the template you'll find in this book to start, grow, raise money for, and ultimately sell the first business I founded. Once I had my first successful exit, my wife and I packed up and bought a house overlooking the Pacific Ocean. From here I've fine-tuned this template, switched some things around, perfected it, and used it to do the whole cycle again.

I've also used it to test business ideas and kill them. A lot of them. Some ideas sound great when you talk about them, or when they're swirling around in your head. But they can change when you start working them out on paper, in a spreadsheet where the numbers have to work, where you can see it outside your head and as importantly see if the business makes sense. You have to be able to solve a problem, market, and sell your product and/or service for a profit.

By using this business plan template to vet ideas, I estimate that I have saved myself millions of dollars, but more importantly I've saved myself years of my life that I could never have gotten back.

One of my crazy ideas actually made sense last year when I worked it through the business plan process and I've now founded another software company. Like me, over 1,500 students have used this template to write their business plans and many have used them as a pitch deck to raise money from investors for their company. Several had never built a business plan, but used this template and raised money with it in a week. I'm not promising you that level of success, but I'm also not ruling it out. Truth is, results vary depending on your business, ambition, dedication, and timing.

What I can promise is that this template has the potential to lead you to building a wildly successful business.

A recent student used the template and raised $1.4 million for her company in four months. Another student had no idea how to build a business plan and had never done one. She followed the steps and was able to recruit a new high value board member for her company. A third student used the elevator pitch template in this book to create a successful marketing campaign.

I'm not saying all this to brag, I'm simply proud of the people who have used my plan to launch and raise money for their businesses. They've worked hard to get their ideas out of their dreams and into the world.

Here's a really cool thing: you can use this modern business plan for any type of business, at any stage: a software business, a service business, consulting firm, e-commerce store, clothing company, product business, drop shipping business, multilevel marketing business, pure affiliate business, media business, restaurant, retail store, real estate, selling courses—you name it and it can be used.

Be brave,

PS: You might notice this book is short. That's on purpose. Making it simple for you took me 20 years.

Three Ways to Get the Most Out of This Book

3. Don't let PERFECT get in the way of GREAT. Your business plan is not static. It's an ever changing, evolving thing. Because of that, perfect isn't going to be possible, so let that idea go right now. Striving for perfect will paralyze you, your goal with this book is to get your plan on paper and get going building your business.

2. Change your SCENERY. Building your plan takes creative and analytical thinking. Changing your scenery will help. If you get stuck on a slide and you're on a flight, get out of your seat and walk up and down the aisle, if you're not- ride your bike, or get up and stretch. Trust the process—it will come to you.

1. Create a CHALLENGE for yourself. For example, if you're reading this on a long plane ride, set a goal to read it and get a draft of your plan by the end of your flight. Or set a three day challenge and mark it on your calendar. It's up to you how you want to divide it up, but plan it, write in on your calendar, and complete your goals.

High Percentage Tips (HPTs) for You

H ere are some things to keep in mind while reading
this book and building your business plan.

It's really a story.

While everyone calls what you're about to build
a business plan, it's really a story. It's your story, and
you want to make it as authentic as possible. People
often try to use language and words that fit into some
style that often strips who they really are right out of
it. Use your words and write how you write, don't try
to be generic or formal. This book will give you a
template to come up with each piece of your
completed business plan, but I'm not dictating your
words. I'm only giving you a template to fit your words
into.

You are unique, as is your team, your ideas for
your business, and your ideas for your products or
services. Let your light shine through when you're

building your plan. The worst thing you can do is try to be something you're not or guess what you think someone else wants by using buzz words and popular slogans. You don't want to be insincere in your business plan.

That being said, don't take this as advice to go so far outside the norm that what you build here and ultimately present to your team, investors, or others, comes across as nuts. I've read business plans that take it too far, and once you cross that line you lose credibility. There's a difference between letting your voice come through and being so far out there that people don't get you. You'll have a feel for what I mean as you work through this.

The main take away is this: Let "you" come through.

You'll be scared.

I'll warn you from personal experience that turning your idea into a business plan may be scarier than you think. You may be saying to yourself right now, "Brandon, why would turning my idea into a business plan be scary? It feels like this is going to be one of the most exciting steps I've ever taken." It might be, but be prepared to feel other ways about it.

Parts of building your business plan can make you feel like your idea may not be a good business after all. You might think the business isn't going to make money or perhaps you didn't have your market as dialed in as you thought you did. Those moments are going to scare the shit out of you because I bet you've built up some confidence that your idea is worth millions, maybe billions.

You've also likely shared this idea with others, maybe only people close to you, but when it appears it might not work you're going to feel your stomach sink and you're going to begin to question everything.

At this moment you may feel like all is lost, that your future is not as bright as you thought, or that all the money you or your company were going to make disappears in an instant. You might feel like your dreams are shattered. You're going to panic and when you do, I want you to remember to keep your nerve, find that place of peace that you have within you, and take a deep breath. That will help you get control of all the stress reactions that just kicked in.

Don't worry, all is not lost. Here's my experience from over two decades of trying to turn different ideas into businesses: there have been times when I went through this exercise and one of the slides seems to showed the business was not going to work. Everything I described above happened, but I kept going and built the other slides and doing so helped to shed some light on whether or not the business could work. Sometimes all I needed to do was make a slight twist to the plan to make it all happen.

If you're lucky enough to build your plan and this never happens, congratulations! You're the outlier and damn lucky. If you get to the end and it turns out the business isn't going to make financial sense, all is not lost. More often than not the idea we set out to build into a business isn't what our end business looks like. You'll be fine and you'll learn about opportunities you didn't know about by going through this exercise with your original idea. This process can lead you to potentially even better, more profitable ideas. Stay strong through the process.

Your business plan is a living, breathing thing.

Your business plan is not static, it's a living, breathing thing that will change as your company grows. The template you're about to learn gives you the skills to get the answers you need as your business grows and as the market changes. Don't be afraid to alter your plan as circumstances change, refer back to the templates and techniques you learn here and you will have the tools you need.

Building your business will be hard at times. Stick with it.

Building a business is hard. If it was easy everyone would do it. At times you will feel alone, you will doubt yourself, you will feel the world is against you, and you might have people rooting against you. These are people who are too afraid to take the risks you are taking. When any of these thoughts happen, just know that it is a normal part of the process. You don't owe anyone comfort on your journey.

You are not alone.

However, you might feel like it at times. Building a company or launching a new product or service can be lonely. You're not alone. Know that there are others just like you embarking on the journey and building companies and launching new products and services. All fellow entrepreneurs have the same feelings at different times during our business-building journey.

And One Final Piece of Advice Before You Start

We'll launch into taking the idea you wrote on the back of a napkin and turn it into a plan after this final piece of advice that comes by way of my late grandmother, Vera.

I believe we remember pivotal moments in our lives like they were yesterday, regardless of our age.

This one is no different. I'm not sure exactly how old I was at the time, maybe 10 or 11, but my brother and I were walking out the door of my grandmother's house to go somewhere. I remember opening the glass door and the lower portion catching slightly on the doorsill because of the humidity. As the door opened, Maryland's humid summer heat hit us in the face while our backs remained protected by the cool air that my grandparents' window units pumped into the house non-stop from June until the end of August.

We were walking up the concrete steps to the car pad and my grandmother looked up and said, "You know you can split the clouds apart if you stare at them and direct your energy."

I remember looking back at my brother with a "What the heck is she talking about?" look and him curiously shrugging his shoulders. He was seven years old and on the brink of learning something new about the world.

She stopped us just before the last three steps that were steeper than the rest and said, "Look up there right now. Pick a cloud. Think hard that you want that one cloud you picked to split apart."

No sooner had I looked up, picked a cloud, and started thinking about it than that stinking cloud broke apart. My brother did the same thing, which again led me to look at him like, "What sort of magic does Mom Mom have?"

Now, to be fair, this was not out of the blue from our grandmother. She was a spiritual person. She had wisdom and downright mystical power about her that's hard to explain, but anyone who knew her could feel it. She ran a consignment shop and people from all over the countryside, far and wide, would come into her shop to get their dose of spiritual fulfillment.

Anyway, she encouraged us to do it again. And you know what, that next cloud did the same thing.

After that second one, she looked at us with confidence and said matter-of-factly, "You can do anything you put your mind to. You just have to believe and channel all your energy into it. Now, let's get going."

My brother and I were amazed. I'm sure you can think back to that time in your life as a kid where you witnessed this sort of magic and you were full of wonder. As I'm sitting here writing this long past the time I should have been in bed, I'm shaking my head because I'm sure you're thinking this was a great teaching moment from my grandmother. I've got news for you, as my mom would say, I actually think my grandmother believed without a shadow of a doubt that we moved those clouds. Not because she wasn't an incredibly smart woman and knew how the wind blew the clouds, but because maybe we actually did!

That unflinching belief that she had in us instilled a lifelong lesson that you really can do anything you put your mind to if you channel your energy with absolute focus. Why not you?!

Get yourself a good cup of coffee or tea if you don't have one already and...

Let's get going!

Slide 1: Elevator Pitch
Get your audience excited to hear about your business.

2   Slide 2: Problem

3   Slide 3: Solution

4   Slide 4: Market Opportunity

5   Slide 5: Go To Market

6   Slide 6: Traction & Milestones

7   Slide 7: Competition

8   Slide 8: Financials

9   Slide 9: Team

10   Slide 10: Funding

11   Slide 11: Summary

Slide 1: Elevator Pitch

If you can't explain it simply, you don't know it well enough.

-Albert Einstein

Your title slide is where you list your company's name, contact info and most importantly, give your elevator pitch.

When you're done, this slide will look like something as simple as this:

Slide 1

```
┌─────────────────────────────────────┐
│                                     │
│   Your Company Name                 │
│        Tag Line                     │
│        LOGO                         │
│                                     │
│   Your Name Phone# email            │
│            website                  │
│                                     │
└─────────────────────────────────────┘
```

HOW TO BUILD THIS SLIDE

This will be the most straightforward looking slide in your entire deck. All you really need to include here is your company name, tagline, logo, and your professional contact information.

What's not written on this slide that you'll still need is your Elevator Pitch. You'll deliver it to your audience while displaying this slide.

Your elevator speech is a short, persuasive speech meant to spark interest in your company, product, or service that gets a conversation started with someone who knows nothing about your business, product, or service.

42

It's not intended to tell your whole company history or even tell too much of anything about yourself. It's meant to hook the listener.

The goal here is to create interest in the company so the person you're talking to becomes engaged. Your elevator pitch should open the door to a follow up conversation that eventually leads to a sale, investment or other desired outcome such as recruiting a new employee.

A great elevator pitch is less than 10 seconds. A good elevator pitch lasts between 15 and 45 seconds. Anything over 45 seconds needs more work.

Here is an example of the evolution of the same elevator pitch so you can compare a great, good and needs work pitch. This pitch is from a company that I founded a few years ago. The great pitch took about a year to get really dialed in. I'm telling you this so you don't get discouraged and you can see what you're aiming for.

A great elevator pitch...

"We help you find files you know you have, but can't find, faster."

A good elevator pitch...

"We hook up to your email and, in a matter of minutes, sort all your files by person, group, company, and in some cases, the place you sent or received them. This allows you to easily find your files and not waste time looking for them."

An elevator pitch that needs more work...

"Hi, my name is Brandon White. I took all my experience from my master's in psychology and combined it with my years of building technology companies to create a SaaS application that hooks up to your email and quickly indexes and sorts all your files by person, group, company, and in some cases the place you sent or received them. This allows you to easily find your files and not waste time looking for them. You can reduce your frustration of wasting time looking for files and do actual work.

I'm very passionate about this because I built it for my wife. I also recruited an amazing team of engineers and they all have master's in computer science and at least 10 years experience."

Getting your elevator pitch dialed in is an ongoing process and it will evolve as your business grows. So don't get discouraged if you don't get it right immediately.

Whatever you do, don't give up. It can be incredibly frustrating, but it's worth it.

Your elevator pitch is a tool you will use in everything you do in your business—in sales, marketing, customer service, recruiting, raising money, HR, and finance.

Before you do the exercise, let's walk through the top three mistakes people make when delivering their elevator pitch so you can avoid them.

1. People start by saying their name.

This is going to sound harsh, but you need to hear it to succeed. No one cares about you. Well, maybe your mom does, but she doesn't count here.

People like to talk about themselves, they like to hear their own names, and they want solutions to their own personal and work problems so that they can save time and make more money.

Lead with their name, if you know it. If you don't know it, ask for it. Then they will have heard their own name twice, once from themselves and once from you. Now you'll have their attention.

2. People give their background.

Here's the deal, you don't have to be "qualified" if you have something that solves a real problem for the person you're talking to. Having a solution to the problem qualifies you.

Sarah Blakely had never made underwear or anything else even close when she invented Spanx. She was selling copiers. Women didn't care. It made them look thin and as far as they were concerned Sarah was a genius.

Don't tell people why you're qualified to solve a problem for them: demonstrate your qualification by offering your solution. That's what establishes your credibility, not a degree nor life experience or a list of accomplishments.

I'll bet you that the person you're talking to will start asking you questions about your product or service once you show you have a solution to their problem.

And guess what? **Now you've changed the dynamic of the conversation from you "selling" to them "buying."**

3. People lead with the story of why they created the company.

People will usually make this mistake either right after they have introduced themselves or right before.

We are passionate about our companies, products, services, and stories. It takes a lot of blood, sweat, and sometimes tears, to create something out of nothing and as a result we like hearing our own story. The problem is that it's a self-licking ice cream cone.

You got it, people don't really care initially. They might ask you why you started your company as a follow up question, **but you have to wait until they ask for you to tell them.** If they do ask, don't spend the next 15 minutes talking. People will get bored and lose interest.

Think about a time when you asked a follow up question like this and someone went into a 15 minute saga. You probably couldn't wait to escape the conversation.

Get your answers down to about 20 or 30 seconds, and no longer. If they keep asking you questions, great. But remember, don't mistake that question for them wanting to hear a 15 minute spiel. They want an interesting story, but a short one.

Remember, **the goal of the entire elevator pitch is to get someone interested in buying your product or service, NOT to hear yourself talk.**

The key here is to practice your elevator pitch AND what you're gonna say if someone asks you questions like:

• How did you come up with X?

• Who's working with you?

- What's your background?

The key to successful elevator pitches is practice, practice, practice. Practice makes progress, not perfect, so stick with it and you'll get there.

> Practice what you will say if someone asks you a follow up question and have a concise response. **Keep it simple and get to the point.**

HOW TO BUILD YOUR ELEVATOR PITCH

Here's the template to get you started right now. I want you to spend 10 minutes or less replacing the words in the brackets with words describing your product. Just get something down on paper to get the ideas flowing.

You know how [adjective describing problem] it is when, [problem]? We make it [adjective describing solution].

Here's another version of the template:

We [verb about solving the problem], [the problem], [adjective about solving the problem] by

....

Toyota Car Dealer:

You know what a pain it is to buy a car? We make it easy with fully transparent pricing and a no haggling experience.

File Finder:

We help you find files you know you have, but can't find, faster.

Barber Shop:

We fix bad haircuts.

Skin Cream:

We take ten years off your age.

Notice how all these spark a level of interest? They do that because they touch on a "pain" point that elicits a follow up question such as:

- "What do you make?

- "How do you do that?

- "How does that work?

- "Where can I buy that?"

Now you give it a shot. Use the following lines to get down your first draft of an elevator pitch.

Your try:

....

....

....

You'll want to keep a log of all the variations that you develop in a word document or note on your computer or phone. You also want to date each of the iterations. This allows you to go back and pull different pieces of past pitches to create different versions of your elevator pitch as your business, product, or service evolves.

Additionally, you can use this record as a reminder of what you were thinking a year ago or three months ago or two years ago.

If you'd like a separate sheet or just a bigger page to work on, you can download and print out this worksheet at

https://BackOfTheNapkinTo.com/BusinessPlan

Best Ways to Practice Your Elevator Pitch

1. Record yourself practicing your pitch on your phone

This way you can play it back and hear how you sound. If this feels awkward and you don't like hearing yourself or seeing yourself on video, that's completely natural. Be brave and have the courage to do it because it WILL make you better and improve your pitch faster.

2. Time yourself.

I like to use a 15 second, 30 second, and 1 minute hourglass. They're good visual tools that make it easy to gauge how much time you have left. The ones that I use are less than $9 on Amazon. You can find them on Amazon by searching for "plastic hourglass timer."

3. See if someone else can remember and repeat it.

One of the **great things about a simple elevator pitch is that everyone in your company can memorize it and become a sales and marketing person.** They'll have the pitch in their back pocket when someone asks where they work and/or what they sell.

SUMMARY

When you show this slide you'll give your elevator pitch and you'll be off to a strong start in your presentation.

The work you've just done is the foundation for all of your other slides. As you build your other slides, your elevator pitch will become clearer and easier to come up with, I promise. Get something down on paper and move on to the next slide. By the end of the book you'll have your elevator pitch dialed in to a good spot.

You kicked this chapter's butt. Let's move forward and tackle your Problem Slide.

You know you nailed
your elevator pitch
when the listener
starts asking you
questions.

1   Slide 1: Elevator Pitch

Get your audience excited to hear about your business.

Slide 2: Problem

What problem are your customers experiencing?

3   Slide 3: Solution

4   Slide 4: Market Opportunity

5   Slide 5: Go To Market

6   Slide 6: Traction & Milestones

7   Slide 7: Competition

8   Slide 8: Financials

9   Slide 9: Team

10   Slide 10: Funding

11   Slide 11: Summary

Slide 2: Problem

Is this a problem
people will actually
pay you to solve?

Your problem slide describes the main problem your customers have that you solve for them with your product or service. It's the foundation that your whole business is built on.

Take your time and make sure you're clearly and simply stating the problem you solve. **No one should be confused about what you do after this slide.**

HOW TO BUILD THIS SLIDE

Three things to remember as you're moving into the main part of your business plan:

1. As you think about the problem you're solving, remember that **it has to be painful enough that someone will pay you to solve it.** We're unapologetically aiming to build a business that makes a lot of money, not a nonprofit. There are

lots of problems that people say they have, but will not pay for. We'll work that out and test it later.

2. Next, you need to know if you're solving an aspirin problem or a vitamin problem. Aspirin problems are things that require urgent solving, vitamin problems are things that would be nice to have, but are not needed. If you're solving an aspirin problem, describing the issue will be a little easier.

Examples of businesses that solve aspirin problems: plumbers, electricians, automation software, hospitals, aspirin itself, other medicines, etc.

If you're solving a vitamin problem it will take a little more work to describe it because you either have to remind someone that what you're solving is actually a problem, or you have to create the problem.

Examples of businesses that solve vitamin problems: fashion brands, high-end clothing brands, jewelry, expensive watches, expensive cars, etc.

What type of problem are you solving?

3. Your plan is a story. We set things up in the Elevator Pitch and now we're expanding on the story laying out the problem.

This slide's template:

1. A person tries to do X.

2. The pain they encounter is Y.

3. Existing solutions are broken or non-existent because of Z.

Your slide can look something like this:

EXAMPLES

File Finder:

1. A person tries to find a file they know they have but can't find.

2. That person gets annoyed, frustrated, and angry that they can't find the file and feel like they are completely wasting their f&^%ing time.

3.   Existing solutions are broken because no one has designed an easy-to-use application that delivers on the promise of finding files faster.

Airbnb example:

1.   Hotels leave you disconnected from a city and its culture.

2.   People feel like they never get an authentic experience and leave a destination feeling unfulfilled.

3.   No easy way exists to book a room with a local homeowner.

Some other things to think about as you're building your problem slide.

Who exactly has this problem?

Men, women, people in an industry, people in a certain demographic? Think about who your customers are.

What proof do you have that people have this problem?

Did you have the problem and decide to solve it? Did you do surveys? Did you read forums where people talk about it? Already have a version of your product that people are paying you for?

What's your MVP?

If you don't have a product or service built yet, what is the most simple, and I mean really simple, version of your product or service that you can build or offer to test if people will pay you?

MVP stands for minimum viable product, and you need to consider this in anticipation for your solution slide.

Use the space below to try working out your problem slide.

If you'd like a separate sheet or just a bigger page to work on, you can download and print out this worksheet   at **https://BackOfTheNapkinTo.com/BusinessPlan**

Fill this in with your information:

The customer you are serving tries or does

....

....

....

The pain they encounter is

....

....

....

Existing solutions are broken because

....

....

....

Now that you've finished figuring out the three pieces of the problem your customer experiences, you just need to put them on your actual slide.

If you feel like this is a really simple way to show the problem, then you're on the right track. It is, and it's meant to be that way. We need to make everything so simple that your grandmother could understand it. Great work on this slide!

SUMMARY

Congratulations, you're another step closer to building the company, product, or service you sketched out on the back of that napkin.

You've opened with your elevator pitch. You've set up the problem. Now you're going to show the solution. (Hint: It's your company, product, or service.)

Let's go.

Slide 3: Solution

If you define the problem correctly, you almost have the solution.

-Steve Jobs

Think of your Solution slide as the second punch of your one-two combination. You set things up with the problem and now you're presenting the solution in the form of your product or service.

The slide's template:

1. **We solve this problem by [solution] and the benefits are [benefits.]**

2. **[Pictures or demo of your product or service.]**

3. **Here's what customers say, "[testimonial]."**

Your slide should look something like this:

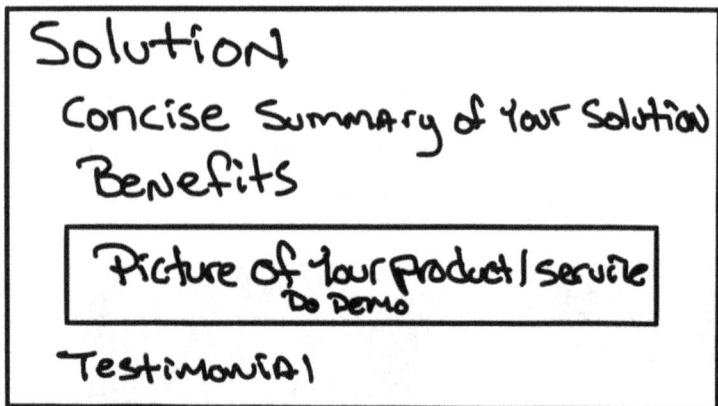

It feels obvious and almost too simple when laid out like this, that's the point. You want your plan and solution to be so simple that anyone can understand. If they understand it, they can buy it.

Ideally, you can describe how to solve the problem in one way. **If you solve the problem in more than one way, don't discuss more than three.** More than three ways and your solution starts getting too complicated to explain. If it's too complicated to explain, it's too hard for potentially interested persons to understand. And too hard to understand means you don't get the response you're looking for. Your customer doesn't buy, your investor doesn't invest, your team member doesn't understand, or you don't get the hire you just spent lots of time and money recruiting.

For the benefits part, stick to three or less as well. If you're saying to yourself, "Brandon, my company, product, or service helps in so many other ways," I hear you, and that is the case with many products and companies. But, if you're only allowed to pick three ways, what are they? Let's go with that for now.

EXAMPLES

File Finder's Solution:

"We solve this problem by automatically sorting all your files by person, company, and topic. Then we of course back them up so you have all of them in one place.

The benefits for you are that you save time by locating files faster and unneeded stress is eliminated by File Finder so you can get done with work at a decent hour."

Airbnb's Solution:

"We solve this problem by offering a web platform where travelers can book a room with a local person.

The benefits to travelers are they save money and are immersed in the local culture."

Something to think about...

Do you remember hearing the old adage, "If you can't simplify a concept down so that a third grader could understand it, you haven't really mastered the concept?"

That's what we're going for here. If it feels hard to do, don't worry, because it is—but it's essential to put the work in. Making something simple to explain means it's easy for your customers to understand. Easy to understand means it's easy to buy your product or service.

If I sound like a broken record saying the same things a few different ways, it's because I really want you to understand the importance of simplicity in this task.

Here are a few things to keep in mind as you build your Solution slide. Jot down some ideas as you go through these questions. You'll finalize all these things in your Traction and Milestone and Financials slide.

1. How am I going to deliver this solution to customers? Are you going to sell it online in a direct-to-consumer (DTC) model? Do you need distributors (a wholesale model)? If you have a service, can you do it remotely or do you need to do it in person? If a combination, what's the split?

2. How am I going to produce this solution? If it's a physical product, how is it going to be made? If it's a service, who do I have to hire?

3. How much am I going to charge for my product or service?

4. What are my milestones to get this solution to customers?

5. What sort of team do I need to deliver my solution?

    Use the space below to start on your solution slide.

If you'd like a separate sheet or just a bigger page to work on, you can download and print out this worksheet at

https://BackOfTheNapkinTo.com/BusinessPlan

Fill this in with your information

We solve this problem by

....

....

....

and the benefits are

....

....

....

Here's what customers say

....

....

....

Your slide should follow this simple template: We solve this problem by X and the benefits are Y. If you feel things are getting too wordy or it feels too complicated, come right back to the template and do your best to streamline.

I have never encountered a single company, product, or service that cannot fit into this template.

Don't work on this slide forever. It doesn't have to be perfect yet, it just needs to be close. As you continue working through more of the slides, you'll clarify your thoughts and that will help you refine your solution.

SUMMARY

We set up your elevator pitch and now the person you're talking to is interested. You've explained the problem people have and have shown that you have a solution to that problem. Next, we're going to talk about how big the market is for your product or service.

Stay strong. Let's go.

Slide 4: Market Opportunity

You conquer your market by starting **local.**

This slide is the first punch of another one-two combination you're going to deliver. In your market opportunity slide you define the size of the market you're going after and break it down into what part of it your product or service will be able to address.

Your slide should look something like the example below. You can also use a graphic like the one on the following page. It does not have to be exactly the same, but you should use a graphic that effectively communicates how you've **identified and narrowed down each of your markets.**

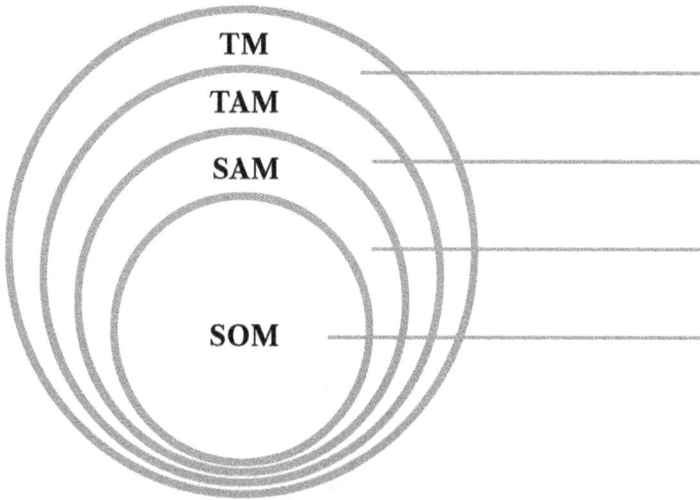

In order to size your market, you'll need to define your TM, TAM, SAM, and SOM.

Total Market (TM) Size

This includes everything in your market.

Example

We'll switch gears from the examples in the last two slides and we'll use a fictitious company called Fishing LuresX, Inc. Let's pretend they make high-end saltwater fishing lures. The total fishing market is worth: $51.1 billion.

This includes all fishing-related expenditures such as travel expenditures, fishing equipment, fishing boats and trailers, and other miscellaneous products.

Copy the process I used to calculate this example to get your market size.

How I Calculated This:

By Googling "size of the recreational fishing market in the United States PDF."

This lead me to an industry report published by the American Sport Fishing Association. The report summarized the market and growth estimates.

Fill in your Total Market size in the graphic in the beginning of the chapter.

Total Addressable Market (TAM) Size

Next, you break down your market further into the subsegment of the market that you can actually address with your product or service.

Example:

Fishing LuresX can't address the Total Market (TM) because it includes more than just fishing lures, such as rods, reels, boats, motors, and clothing.

Looking at only fishing lures, the company has a TAM worth $1,110,875,707.

How I Calculated This:

In the fishing industry report there was a line item under Fishing Equipment Expenditures that listed the amount of money spent on fishing lures.

Just to double check, I Googled "Size of the recreational fishing lure market in the United States PDF." I got a few search results and with a little digging, I confirmed the number in the original report.

Approach it the same way to calculate your TAM, then fill it in on the graphic in the beginning of the chapter.

Segmented or Serviceable Available Market (SAM) Size

Now, break down your market even further to get what part of your total addressable market (TAM) you can serve with your product or service, which is your SAM.

Example:

Fishing LuresX doesn't sell every type of fishing lure under the sun. It sells saltwater fishing lures. The company's SAM is $222,175,141.

How I Calculated This

After some research using Google and using the U.S. Bureau of Economics website, I couldn't find any breakdown of the specific fishing lures market.

To get a solid educated guess of their SAM, I took the total ratio of freshwater anglers to saltwater anglers, which is 1 in 5, and applied it to their TAM of $1,110,875,707.

There are some challenges using this approach because it assumes that freshwater anglers and saltwater anglers spend the same and that lures are priced about the same as well, which may not be true.

But, it has logic behind it and is a best guess. Key in this part of the process is to make sure the logic makes sense and note your assumptions as you make them so you can notate your slide and can remember in six months how you came up with the number.

Following this logic, Fishing LuresX has an estimated SAM of $222,175,141.

Sometimes you'll find this approach is the best you can do, which is fine. You just have to have sound logic behind your approach.

Another way you can get detailed market information is to find a publicly traded company that has a product or service similar to yours and look up their annual report. The report is referred to as a 10-k.

You can find this by going to the company site and looking under their investor section. It's usually posted there or you can look it up at SEC.gov.

Companies will usually break down their market size in these annual reports for investors. The nice thing is that these reports are free to everyone and provide great information.

Figure out your SAM size and fill it in in the corresponding circle in the graphic on the first page of the chapter.

Share of the Market (SOM) Size

Lastly, you're going to break down your market one final time into your Share of the Market or if you're just starting out, your predicted share of the market.

You get to this by thinking about the resources you have, or plan to have, to distribute, market and sell your product or service.

Example:

Fishing LuresX sells fishing lures online in a direct-to-consumer model (DTC). The fishing industry report explains that about 80 percent of all fishing tackle sales now happen online.

This gives Fishing LuresX an estimated market size of $177,740,112. I calculated this number for them by taking 80 percent of their SAM ($222,175,141). But, Fishing LuresX is an independent DTC retailer and it's estimated, based on the report, that big box retailers account for about 75 percent of all fishing equipment sales.

This gives Fishing LuresX a market size estimate of $44,435,028.

Now our fictional company needs to make a guesstimate for how much of that $44,435,028 they can realistically capture.

They can get to this number a few different ways. They can look at where they are going to target their marketing. While they sell online, they can't advertise to every single person. They may decide to target a region, a state or even a city. Or, they could say at this point they plan on capturing 3 percent of this market by X date. This gives Fishing LuresX a SOM of $1,333,050.

As a quick review Fishing LuresX started with a Total Market of $51.1 billion and now has a SOM of $1,333,050.

You may be saying to yourself that this feels like a pretty small share of the market and not a lot of revenue. I agree with you, but remember that this still means selling a heck of a lot of fishing lures. For example, let's assume their average fishing lure sells for $9.99. That means they have to sell approximately 133,438 fishing lures to get to $1,333,050 in sales.

This leads to a very important question that needs to be asked, "How are they going to sell 133,438 fishing lures?!"

You and Fishing LuresX don't need to have this completely figured out right now because you'll be able to further work it out in the coming slides, but it's something to start thinking about.

If you're selling a product, what does your SOM look like and how many units does that mean you have to sell?

If you're selling a service, how many hours do you need to sell/bill to get to your SOM?

How many people does it require given a person works on average 40 hours per week?

Do some quick math and fill in your SOM on the graphic on the first page of this chapter.

Resources to Find Your Market Data

I mentioned a few places to get data in the Fishing LuresX company example, but here's a longer list of resources to check out:

1. Google

Search "[Your Market] industry report PDF" and then keep digging. You'll find some gold nuggets. Sometimes you'll find reports for free because someone is offering it in exchange for your email address or contact information. A cheap price to pay.

2. Industry association websites

Association websites usually have annual reports to promote their industry. They will list them on their site or you can write to them and they're usually very helpful.

3. U.S. Bureau of Economic Analysis

The government tracks everything and there is an amazing amount of free market research data accessible from their website, **https://Bea.gov.**

4. Public company 10-k's, aka Annual Reports

Find a company in your market or very close to it, go to their website and then look for the investor section. Companies will usually have reports listed there. As an alternative, the U.S. Securities and Exchange Commission (SEC) requires public companies to file annual reports with them. The reports are listed on their site in their Electronic Data Gathering, Analysis, and Retrieval system (EGAR). You can access company filings here:

https://www.sec.gov/edgar

5. Independent research firm reports

Usually the research firms will charge for these reports. That being said, they usually provide a solid summary and give good information.

Now you can begin building your customer persona:

Now that you've been through your market opportunity analysis, you can take it one step further and get more specific. This is where you outline who your customers are as individuals.

For the Fishing LuresX company, they know their customer is a saltwater angler. They can further define their customer as saltwater anglers who fish on the East Coast. Or saltwater anglers who fish for marlin. They can get even more specific and say blue marlin anglers who buy their fishing tackle online.

This profile you're building out is often referred to as your customer persona. The more specific you can get, the better your sales and marketing plan will be and the more revenue you'll make. You can have multiple customer personas, but start with one and then as you grow expand them.

Use this customer persona template:

What is your persona's name?

....

What is your persona's background? What is their job?
Do they have a family?

....

....

....

What are the demographics of your persona? Are they
male? Female?

....

....

....

What are your persona's identifiers? What is their
demeanor? What is their communication preference?

....

....

....

What are your persona's primary and secondary goals?

....

....

....

What are your person's primary and secondary challenges?

....

....

....

What can you do to help your customer achieve their goals and overcome their challenges?

....

....

....

What are some real quotes from your persona about their goals and challenges?

....

....

....

What are some common objections as to why your persona would not buy your product or service?

....

....

....

What marketing messaging will you use to reach your
persona?

....

....

....

What elevator pitch will you use for this persona?

....

....

....

**Where does your customer hang out in the
physical world and online?**

This gets some ideas flowing about where you
can advertise and reach your potential customers.

**What marketing message can you give your
prospective customers in your sales and
marketing literature that will attract them?**

TIP: This is the perfect time to reach back, grab your Elevator Pitch, and do another iteration on it because it can serve as the start of your sales and marketing message.

Write a few of your ideas down here:

....

....

....

SUMMARY

Great work! So far you have your elevator pitch, you set up a problem, you showed the solution, and you identified the size of your market. Now you're going to map out how you're going to sell into your market with your Go to Market slide.

Let's go.

If you'd like to print out a bigger copy, you can find a downloadable version of the worksheet here: **https:// BackOfTheNapkinTo.com/ BusinessPlan**

Slide 5: Go To Market

You've identified your potential customers, now what do you want to tell them?

Your Go to Market (GTM) slide is the second punch of the one-two combination that you set up in the last slide. Now that you know your share of the market and who those customers are, you're ready to lay out the details of how you're going to sell your product or service to them.

Think of your GTM plan as the foundation of your sales and marketing plan that you'll add to as you grow your sales and expand into bigger parts of the market.

Your slide will look something like this:

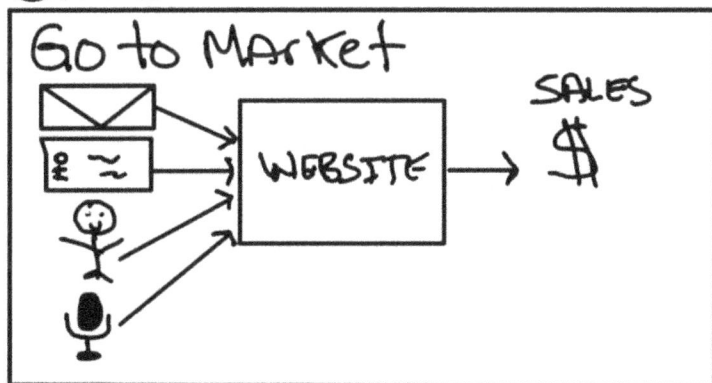

The easiest way to build this slide is to simply map how you envision people becoming customers. This is also sometimes called your customer's journey.

Here's the best part about this slide: you don't have to write any of this out—you can draw it.

You can use this picture as a guide to show each step of your customer's journey as it happens.

Step 1: Attract

Potential customers are out there, and you need to attract them to your product or service to become prospects. You can attract them online through social media posts, blog posts, free lead magnet downloads, free webinars, podcast appearances, articles on you, your product or service, direct mail, TV ads, radio ads, through gorilla marketing like handing out fliers everywhere, or any other creative marketing method.

The key to this stage is that when someone engages with you, be sure to get their contact information. This way you can "market" to them and turn them into a customer.

How are you going to attract customers?

....

....

....

You don't have to nail down the answer to the following question yet, but you need to start thinking about it:

How much money and time is it going to cost you to attract your prospects based on your plan?

Step 2: Engage

Your marketing has gotten a potential customer's attention. Now your sales process kicks in to turn that prospect into a customer by selling them your product or service.

- How is your sales engine going to work?

- Are you going to have a self-serve model?

- Are you going to sell in an email sequence?

- Are you going to call the customer?

- Is your product or service going to be sold and delivered by someone else? A wholesaler, a retailer, a value-added reseller, drop shipper, etc.?

How is your sales process going to work?

....

....

....

You don't have to nail down the following answer just yet, but you need to start thinking about it:

How much money and time is it going to cost you to engage your prospects based on your plan?

Your sales engine closes the deal and now the prospect has turned into a customer.

Step 3: Delight

Now you have to deliver your product or service to the customer. You ideally do it so well that they become promoters of your product or service so you get a word of mouth (WOM) marketing engine going.

How are you going to delight your customers? Never has there been a truer statement than this quote:

"Satisfied customers, touched by positive experiences, never ask... how much it costs."

Think about that for a minute before moving on because if you can delight, you don't have to worry so much about your pricing!

How will you handle customer service? An online form, a number where a customer can reach a human, a chat on your website, something else or a combination of a few of these?

How are you going to delight your customers and make sure they become repeat buyers?

....

....

....

Another question you don't need to have answered just yet, but you need to start thinking about:

How much money and time is it going to cost you to delight your customers based on your plan?

Start Off Small

When you launch your product or service, start off small. There is no way you can launch to your full share of the market (remember, you identified that in your Market Opportunity slide) unless you're planning on having millions of dollars in funding. And even then, it's probably not a good idea to push all your chips in on the first hand.

A better approach is to start really small. Go hyper local and market in your home town or part of a city you live in.

Try all the ideas you outlined above, learn from your mistakes, try again, and make adjustments.

Then slowly push in some more chips, spend more money on marketing, and expand into your market with your proven marketing and sales plans.

Here's the thing: You have to start somewhere that's manageable.

And manageable = starting small.

Tackle a small piece of your market, own it, and use that success to get the next bigger piece of the market.

If you have quick success, you can always increase the speed at which you expand.

Even if you're selling online, a regional strategy is going to serve you better because you can spend targeted marketing dollars specifically in that market. If you pick a market in your community, you can drive to see your prospects and customers, or have get-togethers locally.

The more people hear of your company, product or service the more likely they are to buy. You need to concentrate your efforts so people get to know your company.

In marketing it's called the **Memes Exposure Effect.** Going to the smallest part of the market allows you to focus all your marketing and PR dollars in one area. This provides more exposure to users, thus making them more likely to buy from you.

Even big companies do this. For example, Amazon has a very localized PR strategy they use to push out new offers and features. They have PR professionals in different parts of the county that focus on smaller geographic areas. They use the local PR to drive awareness (aka exposure) and therefore sales. All the local PR adds up to national awareness and the local coverage removes risk for national news outlets to cover stories. The presence of local news interest proves that Amazon's new offers or features are newsworthy to a larger audience.

Listen to former Amazon PR professional Allie Hembree Martin in episode 285 of The Brandon White Show Podcast to learn how Amazon does this.

If it's good enough for a company like Amazon, would it be crazy to suggest it's good enough for you and your business?

EXAMPLES

We'll wrap this slide up with a familiar example. Using the Fishing LuresX company that we used in the last chapter, a go-to-market slide would look like this:

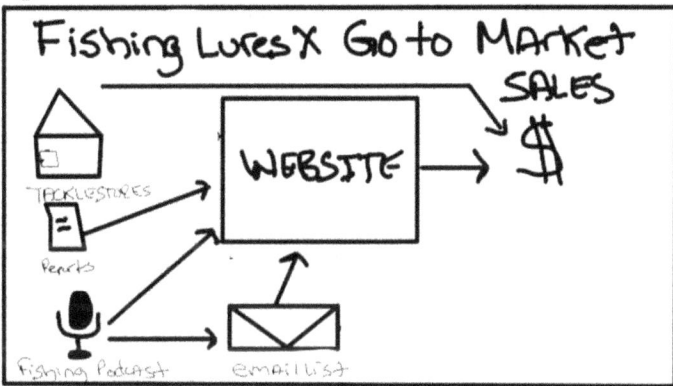

Their GTM is to:

1. Go a wholesale route and aim to land the three independent tackle shops that are within an hour's drive from their headquarters. This will drive awareness and generate some sales. Because they are new, they are willing to have

net 60 terms or even sell on a straight commission basis.

2. Podcast. They are going to do a weekly podcast with local fishing reports, events, and tips. On the show they give the retail shops where they are selling wholesale free publicity and drive sales to the store. This is a win-win. They also drive people to an email list to get a weekly update via email. From that weekly email they advertise their website so the people that aren't going to go to the stores to buy fishing lures can shop on their online site.

3. They are going to fish every week with their lures and catch fish. They're going to take pictures and post them on social media to drive people to their podcast and website.

This is their initial GTM. As they grow, they plan to do some paid ads and sponsorship of fishing tournaments.

By filling out the questions earlier in this chapter, you now have all you need to create your GTM slide. The best way I've ever found is to draw it using one of the two examples outlined in this chapter.

SUMMARY

Nice work with your Go to Market slide! So far you have your elevator pitch, you set up a problem, you showed the solution, you identified the size of your market, and how you're going to advertise and sell into that market. Now you're going to talk about what traction you have and the milestones you need to hit.

Let's go.

Slide 6:
Traction & Milestones

If you don't know where you're going, you'll never get there.

In your traction and milestone slide you're going to outline what traction you have and what your 12 month milestones and goals are for your business.

This is going to set your tempo and narrow your focus for the next year.

Traction is anything that you've done to move your business, ideally sales, forward.

Examples of traction:

If you're just starting up:

- You have a prototype of your product.

- You have people who have given you testimonials of how good your service is. (You did some work for free to get these.)

- You have a distribution deal ready to go.

- You have pre-orders.

- You have an email list with hundreds or thousands of people on it.

- Your website is getting a lot of visitors because of the blog you started.

- You have a patent.

- You recruited a co-founder(s).

- You have a commitment from an investor.

If you already have a business, traction can be:

- You have X in sales.

- You have an existing customer base to sell your new product or service.

- Your website gets a lot of free traffic from your search engine optimization work (SEO).

- You have X distribution partners already in place.

- You're cash flow positive.

- You know your Customer Acquisition Costs (CAC).

- You have a strong word of mouth (WOM) engine happening.

Milestones are the goals you're aiming to hit in the next 12 months. They can be anything from a sales target to hiring certain positions to raising money. The key to your milestones is to be **SPECIFIC.**

This is **NOT** specific:

"I want to increase sales."

This **IS** specific:

"I want to increase our sales from $1.2 million to $1.75 million in the next 12 months."

The specific goal allows you to figure out EXACTLY what you need to do to hit it.

For example, if the Fishing LuresX company sets a milestone to go from $1.2 million in sales to $1.75 million they can now map out how to get there.

They know their average lure costs $9.95. That means they need to sell 50,251 more lures. They know their average revenue per user (ARPU) is $29.85 (three lures) and their customer acquisition cost (CAC) for a new customer is $10.

If their goal is to get all the sales from new customers, they know they need 16,750 new customers (50,251 lures/3 = 16,759)

Because they also know their CAC is $10, they know they're going to need to increase their marketing budget by $160,759 (16,759 x $10 CAC).

They can take this from cash flow if they have that much or they can plan where to get it.

This example illustrates why it's VERY IMPORTANT that you be SPECIFIC with the milestones and goals you set.

Your slide will look something like this when you're done with this chapter.

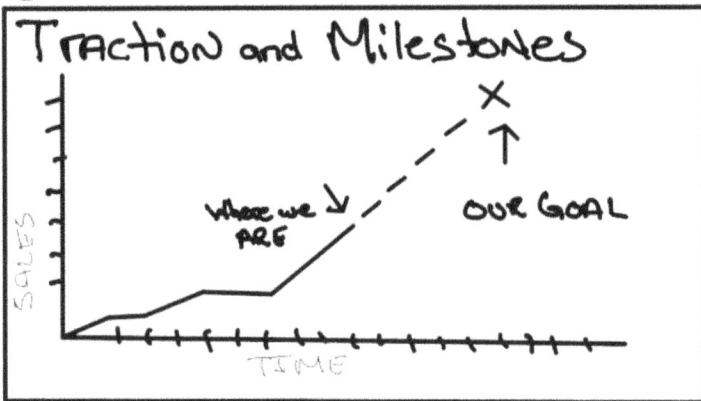

Or it could look like this:

Regardless of the stage of your business, **what traction do you have today** with your company, product, or service this very minute?

....

....

....

If you just started, **do you have a minimum viable product (MVP) or prototype? Have you surveyed people** or businesses that are willing to say that if you make your product they will buy it? Do you have preorders? Write it down:

....

....

....

If you don't really have traction today, **pick the three most important things** for your business to get done and write them down along with a date you want to have them done by. Be very specific, such as:

• "I'll have my business plan done by the end of week."

- "I will talk with 100 potential customers and get their feedback by X date."

- "I will have 100 customers by May 30."

- "I will have $500k in revenue by November 15."

- "I will have five distribution partners by X date."

- "I will have an email list of 500 potential customers by X date."

....

....

....

If you already have your product or service, what traction do you have today?

....

....

....

If you have an online business or are leveraging the online sales channel, what is your growth rate of visitors to your site? Is your length of stay on your site increasing? What is your conversion rate? What is your average revenue per customer (ARPU)? What is your customer lifetime value (CLV)? How quickly is your email list growing? **All of these things are traction.**

....

....

....

What one thing do you need for your business that you don't have today? List it and set a date to get it done.

....

....

....

I'll bet your inclination will be to have a lot of sizzle in this slide, but what you want is real substance that sizzles. **There's a difference.**

Substance is going to get you actual progress and make your business money. Sizzle is going to sound good for a minute until the temperature cools and all you have is cold air and nothing to deliver on.

Using the Fishing LuresX company as an example, here is what a Traction and Milestones slide looks like:

Slide #6

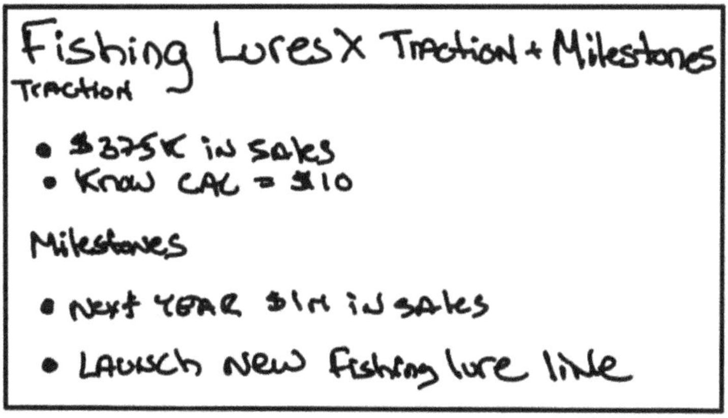

Fishing Lures X Traction + Milestones

Traction

- $375K in sales
- Know CAC = $10

Milestones

- Next year $1M in sales
- Launch new fishing lure line

You don't have to have the answer to this right now, but you need to think about how much money it's going to take to hit your business milestones.

Go back to your notes and estimate how much money you think it will cost to get to each one of your milestones.

Fill in your money estimates and you're done with this slide.

Nice work with your Traction and Milestone slide! You're over half way to the finish line.

SUMMARY

So far you have your elevator pitch, you set up a problem, and showed your solution. You also know the size of your market, how you're going to advertise and sell into that market, and you have your milestones laid out.

Next, you're going to lay out your competition and how you're different.

You've got the momentum going. Keep it up and **let's go.**

Long-term consistency trumps short term intensity.

-Bruce Lee

1   Slide 1: Elevator Pitch
Get your audience excited to hear about your business.

2   Slide 2: Problem
What problem are your customers experiencing?

3   Slide 3: Solution
How do you plan to solve your customer's problem?

4   Slide 4: Market Opportunity
How big is your market?

5   Slide 5: Go To Market
How are you going to address your market?

6   Slide 6: Traction & Milestones
How far have you come and where do you want to go next?

7   **Slide 7: Competition**
Who is your competition and how are you different?

8   Slide 8: Financials

9   Slide 9: Team

10   Slide 10: Funding

11   Slide 11: Summary

Slide 7:
Competition

Don't obsess about them, but know who they are and how you're different.

Identifying your competition helps you strategize how to position your product or service in the market. You don't want to obsess over your competition as you build and scale your company, but it's vital to understand where you stand and how you are different.

When you're done, your slide will look something like this:

Slide #7 1ˢᵗ Example

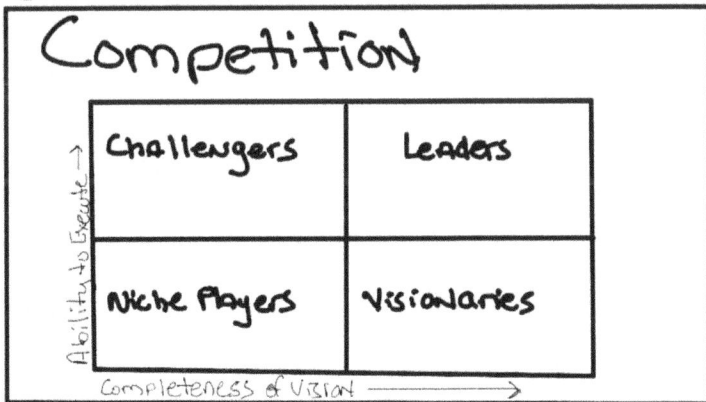

Or this:

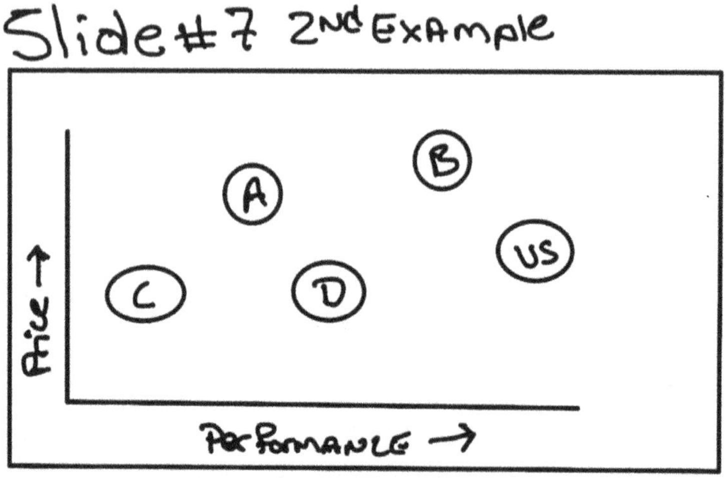
Slide#7 2nd Example
A
B
US
C
D
Price →
Performance →

HOW TO BUILD THIS SLIDE

You build this slide by answering four questions:

1. Who is your competition?

List your competitors (companies, products, and services.) When you do this, think not just about direct companies, products, or services that are your competition, but also indirect competition.

Indirect competition may not be other companies, but be other ways of providing the solution that you offer.

For example, take the company File Finder that we used as an example in the first few chapters. They have software that helps you find files that you know you have, but can't find, faster.

The direct competition is search engines built into other software or hardware products. Their indirect competition is people who organize their files manually. Or people who have executive assistants or junior staff whose job it is to keep things organized. While manual organization is labor intensive, it remains File Finder's indirect competition. Identifying it helps this business not just position their product, but also filter out their target audience.

For instance, they might just say up front in their marketing. "If you're the type of person who has all your files organized and has documentation on how you do it, this product probably isn't for you."

That's a great filter to offer people so they don't waste time looking into a product they don't need and File Finder doesn't spend time and money trying to sell someone something they won't buy.

Use this example and apply it to your product or service and identify your direct and indirect competition.

....

....

....

2. Where is your competition?

Find out where they are: Do they rely on online sales and marketing? Are they in the enterprise part of the market or the small- medium business (SMB) market? Do they only have a physical store and not an online store?

....

....

....

3. How are you different?

It's very important to identify how you are fundamentally different than your competition.

- Does your product/service work better? What does that mean?

- Does your product or service do it faster? Is the speed difference something that matters and really makes you different?

- Are you cheaper? Is being cheaper sustainable to make you different?

- Do you have better customer service? Is it so much better that customers will see you as truly different?

- Is your product easier to use? Is that enough or sustainable as you compete in the market long term?

- Do you have intellectual property (patent, trademark, trade secret) that is going to give you a competitive advantage? If you are relying on this as one of your competitive advantages, how will you allocate money to defend it?

- Do you have certifications that differentiate you from the rest of the companies in your market? Does it take a long time to get these which gives you a head start and/or allows you to see competitors coming?

- Do you or do you plan on having exclusive distribution deals?

List out all of your possible differences that will give you an edge over your competition.

....

....

....

4. What can you learn from your competition?

Are there mistakes your competition is making or has made that you can capitalize on?

....

....

....

5. What are they doing well that you can copy?

....

....

....

Places to Research and Identify Your Competition

Here are some great places you can quickly find and research your competitors:

• **Amazon**

Almost everyone that has a product is selling on Amazon. This makes it easy to find competitive products. Each item lists the brand and/or manufacturer. Google the name of the company or manufacturer to find their website and dig in from there.

- **Instagram**

Almost every brand out there has a social media presence and Instagram is a huge space where people promote products. Instagram users use hashtags to identify the subject or category of their posts. Use the search function and try different keywords to dig around profiles to see what you can find. If you find a brand/company they will usually have a link to their website at the top of their profile page.

- **Pinterest**

Often overlooked because it doesn't get the same attention that Instagram does, but there is a database of posts full of information on all sorts of products. Use the search feature to dig around. A bonus on Pinterest is that almost all the posts have links to take you to the source of the post.

Follow them and dig deeper.

- **Google**

You'll be amazed at what you can find if you do a simple search on "top products/companies in __

Industry." Try different combinations and you're sure to find your competition.

- **Blogs**

There are millions of bloggers out there covering about every market. Search for "Top Blogs in ___ industry."

Tip: At the bottom of the page of a search in Google it will give you suggestions on other search phrases. Try them and see what you can find.

- **Google Maps**

Maps is an especially great resource for those looking to start a brick and mortar business with a local market. Maps has tons of business information searchable by category, e.g., sushi restaurants, pet stores, hardware.

- **Chamber of Commerce**

Chambers are always promoting businesses in their area and usually list them by category on their website.

- **Trade Show Listings**

The event organizers will usually post a list of companies that will be attending to attract visitors. In many cases they will give descriptions of businesses, a bonus for you as you do your research.

- **Research Reports**

We talked about these in your Market Opportunity slide. Research companies publish reports that list the top players in a given industry along with tons of insights into each of the companies and their products. The research firms often charge for these reports. However, in order to entice people to buy the report they will often give an executive summary where you can still get a lot of information.

Tip: A trick I use is if I find a report that costs money, I Google the name of the report and add PDF to the end of the name. Many times this will get me the report for free because someone else bought it and posted it somewhere for whatever reason.

- **Industry Trade Magazines**

Almost every industry has a trade magazine and like clockwork every year, the magazine will run an article listing the "leaders" in the industry. That's gold for you.

There are many different ways and frameworks to break down your competitive landscape. There's a SWOT analysis (strengths, weaknesses, opportunities, and threats), competitive matrix, and other tools. You can find them all, along with instructions on how to use them, in the downloadable resources section at the end of this chapter.

Having said that, now that you have the answers to the above four questions in this chapter you have more than enough insight to get a grip on your competition.

Plus, once you're doing business in your market, you're going to learn in real time as you go up against your competition. That real world experience is going to give you the ground truth to kick your competition's butt.

SUMMARY

Here's how far you've come: you wrote your elevator pitch, you set up a problem, showed your solution, figured out the size of your market and how you're going to advertise and sell to it, you have your milestones set, and you know who your competition is and how you're different.

Now it's time to build your financial model so you can predict how much money you're going to make.

You've kicked this chapter's butt. Keep it up, **let's go!**

Slide 8: Financials

Spreadsheets don't lie.

This is where your business story really comes alive. You're about to get to see how much money you can make with your product or service.

A business plan without financials is incomplete and creates a HUGE risk for you.

Don't skip this slide. I don't want you to lose any time or money on a business idea that is not financially viable.

If you're saying to yourself, "But Brandon, I'm not good with numbers." Not to worry, I make it incredibly simple for you in this chapter.

Your goal is to have a slide that looks something like the below example that projects your revenue and expenses for the next 12 to 18 months.

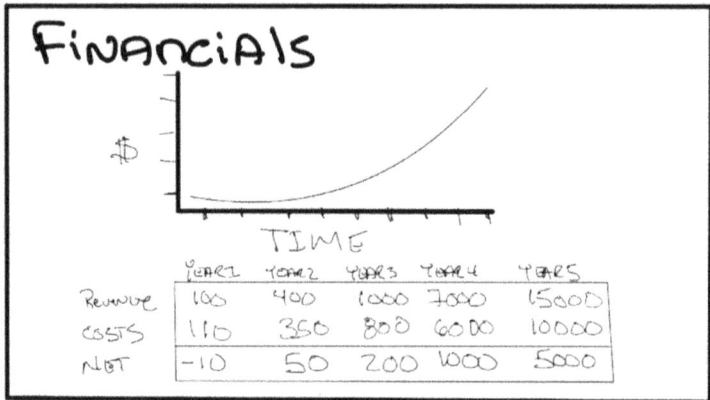

Slide #8

Financials

	Year 1	Year 2	Year 3	Year 4	Year 5
Revenue	100	400	1000	7000	15000
Costs	110	350	800	6000	10000
Net	-10	50	200	1000	5000

One last thing before we continue, doing your financial models in a book is hard because nothing is automated for you. I've created fill-in-the-blanks and workspaces for you if you want to keep it in the book. You can do the work in the spaces provided and then use the link to access the template at the end of the chapter and fill in your answers on your computer.

HOW TO BUILD THIS SLIDE

If you have your computer nearby, I highly encourage you read this chapter in front of it. This way you can use the template and fill in the blanks on the spreadsheet as you read the chapter.

The choice is yours. My aim is to make this as easy and painless as possible for you.

There are three financial documents that you need to be aware of. Don't worry you're only going to build one for this slide. They are:

1. Profit and loss statement

2. Cash flow statement

3. Balance sheet

For your financial slide we're only going to focus on producing one of these. Let me tell you a quick story to emphasize why. When I started my first company, Tom—the same Tom from the first chapter of this book—introduced me to a lawyer, Harry Glazer, whom I remain friends with to this day. At the time he was partner at Greenberg Traurig law firm.

I walked into his office and within the first 10 minutes of meeting him, after some pleasantries, he said, "Kid, it sounds like this is your first time doing a venture-backed start up. Of all the advice I'll give you, this acronym is the most important: DROOFM. Don't run out of f *#king money."

I've never forgotten that advice.

Cash is king. Those are the rules, and because of that, we're going to focus on building a cash flow statement first.

The profit and loss statement and balance sheet are very important financial documents; we just don't need them quite yet.

We're keeping it simple. You'll hire an expert to help you with the other documents down the line. And in the early days if you do your own accounting, or have a bookkeeper to help you, your QuickBooks account will produce these for you.

It's also worth mentioning that there are many issues in finance such as depreciation, different types of accounting methods, ways to create 401(k) programs that can literally save you hundreds of thousands a year, and other finance and tax strategies that we are not going to cover. They are very important, but they're for another book.

And here's the thing, it's a great problem to have, to need to hire a professional to advise you on these things when the time comes. It means you're selling your product or service and your business is throwing off a profit that's landing in your pocket.

So when you tell someone about this book and some finance whiz says to you, "Oh, the author didn't teach you about X, Y, and Z," just ignore them.

The goal here is to teach you how to get a basic grasp on the economics of your business and what it's going to cost for you to achieve a cash flow positive status and from there, scale your business to profitability.

Let's jump in.

Your cash flow statement provides information regarding all cash inflows your company receives from its ongoing operations and external investment sources, as well as all cash outflows that pay for business activities and investments during a given period.

A key point to understand is that just because revenue shows up in the profit and loss statement does not mean the company actually has the cash.

Why?

Well, let's say you sell to retailers. You invoice them, which means you made a sale, but they have 30 days to pay, that means you don't have the actual cash yet.

You care about cash.

Or say you sell on Amazon or Shopify, they may not pay you immediately because they hold for things like bad charges or returns.

So while you are booking sales, you do not have hard cash in your bank account to use yet. To bridge that gap you might get a line of credit from your bank, or you might raise some money from investors.

This is why it is vitally important to manage your business on a cash basis, not a P&L basis.

> **Start by answering the following questions about your cost of goods sold:**

How much will you sell your product or service for? E.g., $29.99 for a product, $150 per hour for a service.

....

....

....

How many or much of your service will you sell in each of your first or next 12 months?

....

....

....

Tip: Your sales are going to increase each month. For example, if you think you're going to sell 120 units in the first year, don't take 120 and divide that by 12 to get 10 units a month. You might sell two units the first month, three the second, and so on. Assume sales are going to ramp up.

Tip: If your product is seasonal, make sure the units sold are in the month that you have seasonal sales.

Fill in your predicted units sold below:

Month 1	Month 2	Month 3
Month 4	Month 5	Month 6
Month 7	Month 8	Month 9
Month 10	Month 11	Month 12

What will it cost you to produce your product or service?

....

....

....

Tip if you have a product: Include all the costs. Meaning if you are going to make it overseas, think about the product, packaging, import fees, transportation fees, and storage fees. If you are going to accept credit card payments, estimate how much it will cost you. On average you can expect to pay 2.5 percent of the total price plus $0.25 per transaction.

Tip if you have a service: How much are the people that produce this service going to cost you? This includes a base salary, bonus, taxes you pay on their salary, health insurance, 401(k) matching, their equipment if you have to initially buy them a computer, tools, or other equipment.

NOTE: IF YOU ACCEPT CREDIT CARDS

Just because you take credit cards doesn't mean that you are going to get paid right away. If you accept returns and/or start executing a high volume of transactions, card processors will often hold back some of your money that you made for 30, 60, or even 90 days because they want to have money to return to customers for refunds if needed. Keep this in mind when you're building your financials.

If you have to produce a minimum number of units from your manufacturer, what are your initial order costs? It's going to cost you cash upfront to buy the inventory.

....

....

....

General and Administrative Expenses

Office

If you plan on having an office, how much is it going to cost you per month for rent?

Month 1	Month 2	Month 3
Month 4	Month 5	Month 6
Month 7	Month 8	Month 9

Month 10	Month 11	Month 12

Utilities for your office

Month 1	Month 2	Month 3
Month 4	Month 5	Month 6
Month 7	Month 8	Month 9
Month 10	Month 11	Month 12

Sales and Marketing

Tip: This includes the cost of your website creation, monthly hosting, anyone you have to hire, events you may attend, shows you may attend, paid ads, and any other sales and marketing costs. This does not include the cost of sales people. That will be accounted for in your Salary section.

Month 1	Month 2	Month 3

Month 4	Month 5	Month 6
Month 7	Month 8	Month 9
Month 10	Month 11	Month 12

Software & Hosting

Any and all software and hosting expenses.

Tip: This includes things like Google Workspace or Microsoft 365 that has all your email accounts, document cloud storage, your website hosting, CRM software you use to manage your customers, email marketing software if separate from your CRM, and accounting software like QuickBooks.

Month 1	Month 2	Month 3
Month 4	Month 5	Month 6
Month 7	Month 8	Month 9
Month 10	Month 11	Month 12

Hardware

You want to keep things like computers and printers separate because not all hardware can be written off as an expense from a tax perspective in the first year. Your accountant will be able to sort this for you at the end of the year. In the meantime, you care because it will cost you cash to buy the hardware.

Month 1	Month 2	Month 3
Month 4	Month 5	Month 6
Month 7	Month 8	Month 9
Month 10	Month 11	Month 12

Salaries

If you're going to hire people as W2 employees (versus contractors) whom do you need to hire? And what about:

- Their base salary?

- Their bonus, if any?

- How much of their health insurance you will cover?

- What 401(k) percentage you will match?

- The portion of the taxes you pay Uncle Sam on their salary (estimate 7%).

Tip: If you're not absolutely sure of all the costs, estimate them. Also, refer to the online resources at the end of this chapter to guide you.

Position 1 Title, Cost, Month you will hire them:

....

Position 2 Title, Cost, Month you will hire them:

....

Position 3 Title, Cost, Month you will hire them:

....

* If you have more people, use a separate sheet of paper or the template I made for you. You can find the link to get to it at the end of the chapter.

Monthly total cost of your team

Sum up your team costs. Note which months people will start if they don't all start at Month 1.

Month 1	Month 2	Month 3
Month 4	Month 5	Month 6
Month 7	Month 8	Month 9
Month 10	Month 11	Month 12

Professional Services

These include your accountant, lawyer, graphic artists, consultants, and/or contractors.

Workspace:

....

....

....

Monthly totals:

Month 1	Month 2	Month 3
Month 4	Month 5	Month 6
Month 7	Month 8	Month 9
Month 10	Month 11	Month 12

Office Supplies

This includes things like printer paper, pens, paper, and staples.

Month 1	Month 2	Month 3
Month 4	Month 5	Month 6
Month 7	Month 8	Month 9
Month 10	Month 11	Month 12

Insurance

Whether you sell a product or service you need to have insurance. Estimate $150 per month if you're not sure so you have something allocated for it as a placeholder.

Month 1	Month 2	Month 3
Month 4	Month 5	Month 6
Month 7	Month 8	Month 9
Month 10	Month 11	Month 12

Travel

You'll want to include transportation and hotels for any travel you predict you'll need, such as visiting potential customers and suppliers or attending conferences.

Month 1	Month 2	Month 3
Month 4	Month 5	Month 6

Month 7	Month 8	Month 9
Month 10	Month 11	Month 12

Meals

You'll include eating out with clients and meals while traveling. Some business owners combine meals with travel. I don't recommend this because not all meals are 100 percent tax deductible. Many meals are only 50 percent tax deductible, which means if you combine them with travel in your accounting, you will spend hours at the end of the year separating them. Extra credit if you can guess how I learned that one. ;-)

Month 1	Month 2	Month 3
Month 4	Month 5	Month 6
Month 7	Month 8	Month 9
Month 10	Month 11	Month 12

Telephones

You'll include any business numbers or lines and cell phones you use for work for you and your team. Remember that if you have to buy a new phone, include that cost in the month(s) where the cost is incurred.

Month 1	Month 2	Month 3
Month 4	Month 5	Month 6
Month 7	Month 8	Month 9
Month 10	Month 11	Month 12

Miscellaneous

This is a catch-all for things you didn't remember or for estimates that were off.

Tip: I generally take 5% of all the expenses and use that as my miscellaneous input. You would rather come in lower on expenses than have to come up with cash you didn't plan for.

Month 1	Month 2	Month 3
Month 4	Month 5	Month 6
Month 7	Month 8	Month 9
Month 10	Month 11	Month 12

What to do next...

Now that you have your estimates of your expenses you need to download the Excel spreadsheet or copy the Google Sheets workbook I built for you and input your numbers.

The chart is automated for you so you can use it on the slide, if you choose.

If you would rather build your financials from scratch feel free to do so. You can use the template I made as an example to copy. All the templates accessible so you can see how I built the whole sheet.

Once you have your estimates in a spreadsheet, you will be able to see exactly what your business looks like. Now you know how much money you think you'll make and your company's expenses along the way.

One of the major numbers you want to put on your slide is how much it's going to take to start your business. You'll be able to see that by looking at the bottom of your cash flow statement. This is a key number for you.

About your numbers...

If your numbers work, meaning your revenue exceeds your expenses and you can make a profit at some point in your projections, congratulations.

If your numbers don't work out of the gate, **don't worry.** This is the point of building your financials.

Play with the numbers until they work. They may not work exactly how you had them in your head and that's okay. Adjust them until you get to a place that feels close and viable.

At the end of the day, not all businesses make money in the first few months or even the first year. The real question is can your company eventually make a profit and how much time and money is it going to take you to get to that breakeven point?

If you discover through this exercise that you're going to need to raise money, that's fine. The good news is that you're really close to getting your business plan completed. With it, you'll be able to take it and move to the next phase of your process, raising money.

Once you figure out your numbers and get this slide done, there are only a few things left to iron out. Then, we'll address raising money with your plan in the funding chapter.

Business is serving your customers and making money doing it. Your financials are an absolutely vital tool that guides you in your ability to do that.

NOTE: If after trying to build your financials it's not going well or you're just over it and want someone to do them for you, check out the books resource center here, **https://BackOfTheNapkinTo.com/BusinessPlan**, where I give you some options to get help or have them done outright for you at a reasonable cost.

SUMMARY

Here's an update on how far you've come:

You have your elevator pitch, you set up a problem, you showed your solution, you know the size of your market, how you're going to advertise and sell into that market, you have your milestones set, you know who your competition is and how you're different, and now you have your financial model and can predict how much money you're going to make and how much it's going to cost you to get to profitability.

This was a hard slide, but you got through it.

You're on the home stretch. Next up, your team.

Let's go!

This is your business plan in numbers.

If you'd like to print out a bigger copy, you can find a downloadable version of the worksheet here: **https://BackOfTheNapkinTo.com/BusinessPlan**

Slide 9: Team

There's no replacement for **top talent.**

Now we're ready to talk about your team who, along with you, are going to execute your business plan. This slide talks about the team you have and the positions on the team you'll need to fill.

The good news is that you already have some of this work completed from your Finance slide.

Remember how you mapped out people and when they would come on board? That's going to come into play here.

Your company, regardless of its stage of evolution, needs a strong team. You need passionate, driven, and highly skilled people.

If you're just starting out and have limited resources, you'll be tempted to settle for someone who will work for now. Even if you can't afford the level of skill you need or you're just anxious to get started, **don't compromise on your team members.**

Here's the deal, building a business is hard and the statistics say that no matter how good your product or service is, the odds are against you.

Because of this, you need to control every variable that you can control.

In this case, that means being strict on hiring team members. You can't afford to waste time managing a bad egg or waste money paying them to do work they're not getting done.

Your slide will look something like this when it's done:

HOW TO BUILD THIS SLIDE

Answer these questions:

Who is on your team today?

....

....

....

What are each of their skills/titles?

....

....

....

What positions do you need to fill in three months?

....

....

....

What positions do you need to fill in six months?

....

....

....

What positions do you need to fill in 12 months?

....

....

....

Are you going to have an advisory board?

....

....

....

If yes, who do you need on it? Think skills and then people who have those skills that you might already know or need to recruit.

Advisor highlights:

- They are not legally bound to the business.

- They will help you because they like you.

- They may be compensated with equity, dinners, drinks, and gratitude.

....

....

....

Who is on, or needs to be on, your Board of Directors?

Highlights of what a Board of Directors can do to help you build your business include:

- They are legally bound to the business.

- They have different areas of expertise to help you.

- They are a mix of investors and independent members.

- They will cost equity and/or cash.

Your notes:

....

....

....

Whom do you want to have on your Board? Just like your advisors, think skills and then people.

....

....

....

NOTE: While building this slide, you may discover a few positions that you didn't think about when you were building your financials. After you've done this slide, go back and update your financials. You didn't make a mistake, it's part of the process.

Hiring Framework

Here's the framework I've developed for choosing team members over the last two decades of building companies. It will get you started. Use and modify it as you want for your company.

Overarching idea: "Selection is an ongoing process."

This means that being selected as part of the team doesn't give you the right to be on the team.

Everyone earns their position, daily.

But, not everyone is going to be on their game all the time. However, major or prolonged lapses are cause to be let go.

The 12 traits I look for when hiring people that you can use as a guide.

People aren't perfect, but you want people to have at least 89 percent of each one of these. If you accept less than that, the risk of a bad team member increases exponentially.

1. Self-Teaching and Problem Solving

Person must be a self-starter. Able to do research and teach themselves how to do something by finding instruction and learning without a "structured" environment and without being told to do so.

2. Introspection, Self-Reflection, Judgment

Must be able to look within with an honest lens, critique themselves to improve. Able to hear and apply criticism.

3. Bias Toward Action

Better to make a decision than none at all.

4. Subordinate to the Mission/Goal

The mission of the company to succeed is bigger than themselves and even when they disagree (see #10), if voted against, they fall in line and do not have a "I told you so" attitude.

5. Comfortable with Ambiguity

Able to work in and thrive in ambiguity.

6. Honesty

With others and themselves.

7. Physical Health

Values being healthy and recognizes the benefits. Understands their own needs and how health affects all areas of their life.

8. Tenacity

Understands there are times when the mind will want to give up, but they have the will to push through, to keep going.

9. Risk Tolerance—Be Brave

Willing to take risks and make mistakes with the confidence they can fix it and find a correct path.

10. Willing to Challenge Authority

Willing to speak up when they don't agree.

11. Respect for Others

Respects people as humans.

12. Will Ask for Help When They Need It

Asking for help is hard sometimes. You want a person who knows when they're spinning their wheels and will ask for help.

Tip: Know your gaps and fill them in.

SUMMARY

Understand your strengths so you can offset your weaknesses. You need to be brutally honest with yourself here. There are some weaknesses that you will overcome: for example, if finance is not your thing, know enough to be able to ask questions, which you should by now after your Finance slide. Don't try to do your taxes or finance strategy, get a professional to help you.

Some things you are never going to be able to overcome. That's not a bad thing—it's who you are. If you are not a great manager, but you're a great visionary, find someone who can run projects for you. Even Mark Zuckerberg realized this, which is why he hired Sheryl Sandberg.

Be honest and find people who can fill in your gaps, not necessarily duplicate your strengths.

TIP: Starting a business or launching a product or service within a company can be a lonely job. Find a peer group and join, even if it costs you some money. I've found the value and support is 10x whatever the cost.

Your team is key to your business's success and now you have a plan to build yours.

Here's how far you've come:

You have your elevator pitch, you set up a problem, you showed your solution, you know the size of your market, how you're going to advertise and sell into that market, you have your milestones set, you know who your competition is and how you're different, you have your financial model and can predict how much money you're going to make and how much it's going to cost, and now you have your team and a plan to build your team.

You have two more slides left. Next up, is your Funding slide. **Let's go!**

Team culture starts on day one.

Slide 10: Funding

Investors require business plans. It's not open to negotiation.

This slide explains how much money you need to start, launch, or grow your business. You already have a head start on building this slide because you know the amount of money you need from your financials slide.

Your slide will look something like this when you're done:

Slide # 10 Example

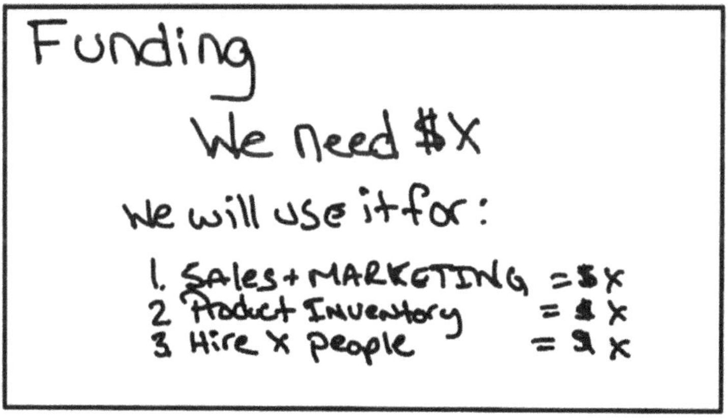

Funding

We need $X

We will use it for:

1. Sales + MARKETING = $X
2. Product Inventory = $X
3. Hire X people = $X

HOW TO BUILD THIS SLIDE

How much money do you need to get your business started and run it for 12 months?

....

....

....

How much of that amount do you have right now?

....

....

....

If you need more than you have right now, where do you plan on getting the funding? (Hint: a bank, credit cards, friends and family, angel investors, venture capitalists, preorders.)

....

....

....

It's really no more complicated than that. If you're saying something like, "Brandon, it sure sounds simple but, I need to raise money for my company, and that's hard."

Raising money can be hard, but it can also be easy with a great plan—a plan that you have almost completed now with a little guidance on how to do it. I've put together some resources for you on the website that accompanies this book, to help you.

If you're funding the company yourself through your existing business or savings, that's awesome. But I still suggest that you take the time to really understand your monthly funding so there are no surprises.

SUMMARY

You have your elevator pitch, you set up a problem, you showed your solution, you know the size of your market, how you're going to advertise and sell into that market, you have your milestones set, you know who your competition is and how you're different, you have your financial model and can predict how much money you're going to make and how much it's going to cost, you have your team and a plan to build your team out, and now you have a plan for funding your business.

You have one more slide left. Next up, is your Executive Summary slide.

Let's go!

DROFM.
Don't run out of
f$%!king money.

Slide 11: Summary

This is your
business plan
in 1 page.

Here's some great news for you: you already have every single thing you need to put this slide together. Your Executive Summary slide is nothing more than a summary of each of your other slides. It brings your whole business story together in one place.

This slide serves multiple purposes, they include:

1. You can use this one pager to send to people who are interested in your company.

2. If you're presenting your business plan to your team, prospective employee, or investors, it brings everything together so they remember all the important points. By the time you've gotten to this slide in your presentation, you're probably at minute 30 of your meeting and people forget. This slide presents your businesses' essential characteristics in one place.

Your slide will look something like this when you're done:

Slide # 11 Example

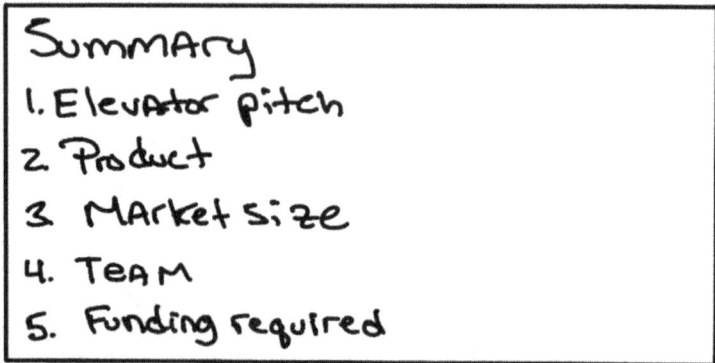

Summary
1. Elevator pitch
2. Product
3. Market size
4. Team
5. Funding required

HOW TO BUILD THIS SLIDE

The first thing is to put your shortest version of your elevator pitch at the top. Then, summarize the biggest take away from slides two through 10 and boil it down to the fewest words possible. Phrases and bullet points are fine for this slide.

Your goal here is to give someone who reads this your most important points. You're boiling your plan down to the very essentials.

Tip: You should be using at least a 32-point font on this slide. People need to be able to read it. Also, you don't want people reading your slide while you're talking—that's what happens if you write in a 10-point font and try to get every last feature in. You want people to listen to what you are saying. The phrases in this slide are simply prompts to remember the larger idea of that section of your plan.

This slide is your executive summary and a reminder of the main points of your business plan for anyone you're presenting it to. It also narrows things down to the very essentials, which makes it easy for you to convey your message and for others to understand it.

SUMMARY

Here's how far you've come:

You have your elevator pitch, you set up a problem, you showed your solution, you know the size of your market, how you're going to advertise and sell into that market, you have your milestones set, you know who your competition is and how you're different, you have your financial model and can predict how much money you're going to make and how much it's going to cost, you have your team and a plan to build your team out, you have a plan for funding your business, and now you've wrapped it all up nicely in your summary slide.

Conclusion

Congratulations on finishing your business plan!

You now possess your roadmap for your business. The next step in your journey is hands-on execution. You'll make mistakes along the way, but that's a good thing. It means you're doing things, trying things, making it happen, and most importantly learning what works for you and your business.

Your business plan is a living, breathing, changing thing. I suggest you revisit it on a monthly or at the least a quarterly basis and update it with the things you've learned. It will act as a good review and map for your road ahead.

You have a great future ahead of you and I wish you the very best of success. I'm in your corner rooting for you!

Acknowledgements

It can be overwhelming when you sit down to write an acknowledgements page and realize just how many people have been involved in your journey. I know I'm going to forget someone who should not be forgotten. If you're that person, I'm sorry.

It's taken me almost a year to get this book written and there have been several versions of it along the way. The early versions were not that good. The usefulness and simplicity of this book are a result of the feedback and encouragement of many people.

This book would never have come to fruition without the help and patience of Gia Beverati who endured my procrastination, endless changes, and new ideas over the last year. She's informed me that this book process has been responsible for some new grey hairs. Me cause anyone grey hairs?! Come on man! I blame age.

Also, my wife Ivette, who has been patient reading and rereading pieces over the last several months and listening to all the new ideas I've had for material to include. This will likely be the one time I acknowledge that I may have sounded like a parrot repeating myself regularly to work many of the ideas and concepts.

Others include:

Marty Strong, whose mentorship, manuscript review, editing, and advice on all things to do with writing a book has been irreplaceable.

Shanti Henderson, whose inspiration of having written over 20 novels by age 15 has kept me going trying to get just one book done. Also, her advice and direction around publishing and promotion has helped me avoid countless mistakes.

My mom, who has provided some great suggestions around how to get the book out there even when I didn't want to hear it because I was frustrated just getting the book written in the first place.

Our professional editors who provided candid feedback and simply made this book better.

Beth Winter who read through numerous versions and gave invaluable feedback on a stream of cover ideas.

All the other friends, family, and strangers who read early drafts of the book and provided feedback. All of your advice has made this book so much better than what it was when I started.

All the people on my email list that pre-ordered the book and provided comments along the way as I published chapters in my weekly emails.

And anyone else I'm forgetting, thank you!

About Brandon White

Brandon White has a gift for distilling seemingly complex ideas into practical, easy to use knowledge to help people get the very best out of their time, talent, and ideas.

People regularly tune into the top-ranking podcasts he hosts to get a weekly dose of new ideas and actionable information to help them win in business and in life. Brandon's most well-known podcast is The Brandon White Show boasting over 475 episodes.

From celebrity status entrepreneurs like Steve Case, founder of AOL, thought leaders like Chris Hood, who heads Business Innovation and Strategy at Google, to Special Forces operators, National Geographic Explorers of the Year, professional athletes, and seemingly ordinary people doing extraordinary things, The Brandon White Show has had them all.

Photo Credit: DSU 2023

Brandon is also the founder and CEO of File Finder, a SaaS application software company that helps you find files you know you have, but can't find, faster.

He started his professional career in technology as a pioneer on the Internet in 1996 as the Founder/CEO of Worldwide Angler, Inc. Worldwide Angler was recognized as the #1 social networking and e-commerce site for sport fisherman on the internet. He sold the company to VerticalScope (XTSE: FORA) in 2012.

He's a sought after speaker on emerging technology, entrepreneurship, and the internet and has taught over 1,500 students his template to build a business plan and pitch deck in 11 slides.

He lives Half Moon Bay, CA with his wife and dogs, and when not at keyboard can be found zipping up and down the California coast on his road bike.

You can find out what Brandon's up to at the moment at https://BrandonCWhite.com

Back of the Napkin to... is a book series that's designed to keep seemingly complex things simple, real, and focused so readers get what's required in an easy to implement solution that they can get it done on a flight from San Francisco to New York.

We've come to find out that even with these solutions some people simply want it done for them so they can move to the next stage of process.

Whether that's building a business plan, full-scale business financials, a pitch deck to raise money from investors, a marketing plan, or other topics of our books.

If you want to shortcut the process we have that solution too.

Visit **BackOfTheNapkinTo.com/services** to learn more.

www.ingramcontent.com/pod-product-compliance
Lightning Source LLC
Chambersburg PA
CBHW021459180326
41458CB00051B/6883/J